THE *ORIGINS* OF *PROLETARIAN* *POETICS*

Spiderwize
Remus House
Coltsfoot Drive
Woodston
Peterborough
PE2 9BF

www.spiderwize.com

A CIP catalogue record for this book is available from the British Library.

ISBN: 978-1-912694-86-0

THE *Origins* OF *Proletarian* *Poetics*

NIGEL PEARCE

CONTENTS

INTRODUCTION:

A World To Win?

The rationale for this book was that my interest in the relationship between Lord Byron and John Clare had been set on fire. However, I wanted to explore what happened when the poor became organized in the light of Romanticism. Discovering the autodidactic tradition of the Chartists was important. Here were a collectivity of poor poets who did not lose their sanity but actively contested both poetically and politically the dominant literary terrain. The problem my book's title sets up to be solved is simply this. To what extent was the flowering of British labouring-class poetry during the period of Chartism, 1836-52, to be seen to have evolved and differentiated itself from Romanticism and the other dominant mode of poetry of the epoch, the dramatic monologue? Did this poetry become an autonomous class literature? Indeed, is the latter possible under the conditions of capitalism? I shall have to provide an explanatory framework to show how and why poetry was a dominant form in the proletariat while it was becoming marginalized in the mainstream. The novel would become the favoured reading of the middle- classes. Nevertheless, some Chartist prose was written, but does not stand reasonable comparison with the sustained and diverse body of Chartist poetry.[1] The poetry was, with few exceptions, written by working men and women who would have had little or no access to the rules and norms of 'form' other than from assimilating them through what they had read or heard rather than through formal education. I shall understand the solution to my conundrum will lie in a qualitatively different society, one not based on commodification. Thus, my contention is that it was in the form and the material conditions of its composition which made Chartist poetics counter-hegemonic. The puzzle is complicated once the veil of ideology is removed as Marx delineated:

> *The ideas of the ruling class are in every epoch the ruling ideas, i.e. the class which is the ruling material force of society, is at the same time its ruling intellectual force. The class which has the means of material production at its disposal, has control at the same time over the means of mental production, so that thereby, generally speaking the ideas of those who lack the means of mental production are subject to it. The ruling ideas are nothing more than the ideal expression of the dominant material relationships...* [2]

We understand that beyond the veil of material inequality lay one of mental disparity. By challenging that Chartism contested the very heart of bourgeois culture. Indeed, for their endeavour to succeed they would have needed to put a stake through it. Marx twice intended to write a treatise on aesthetics but on both occasions failed to complete it. Hence the breadth of Marxist aesthetics. My position is that the two analytical instruments of the Marxist project, historical materialism and dialectical materialism, must provide the methodology and illuminate the

---

1   *The Literature of Struggle: An Anthology of Chartist Fiction [ed] Haywood, Ian London, Routledge, 1995).*

2   *Marx, Karl & Engels Frederick The German Ideology (London, Lawrence & Wishart, 1982) p, 62.*

social circumstance of any attempt to arrive at a meaningful understanding of the relationship between class and literature. In a late letter Engels hinted that the Formalist project is not a blind alley as Plekhanov argued. The latter is the father of a crude Marxist 'Reflectionism' in matters of society and literature. Rather Engels, by arguing as (Hemingway, 2005, p.3) makes clear 'different spheres of intellectual production have what Engels call 'inherent relative independence.'[3] Nevertheless, given these caveats we can understand that Chartist writers were connected to a mass movement which Lenin called: 'the first genuinely mass revolutionary movement', 'the word but one before Marxism. That the unique and cross-generic nature of the original primary material was a 'counter-hegemonic' questioning of an emerging and multifaceted bourgeois narrative.

I will focus on Thomas Cooper and Ernest Jones who had very different social and ideological trajectories within Chartism, both wrote voluminously. Also, they were incarcerated for being leaders of Chartism, Thomas Cooper in 1842 and Ernest Jones in 1848. I show the reasons for the failure of Chartism and, therefore, a counter- hegemonic British labouring-class poetic and argue that for proletarian writers to thrive a society based on 'use-value' rather than 'exchange value' is necessary. Where the masses have control of the material 'means of production'. The work of William Morris on aesthetics is significant but, I argue, limited. I also venture that the ideas of Boris Arvatov and some around the short-lived Soviet avant-garde like Bogdanov were persuasive as they sought to create a 'laboratory for pure proletarian ideology.'[4] Lenin criticized this school of thought, Prolecult, which was a Left art movement aiming at the creation of a new art and literature. One which was collectivised because the proletariat is a collectivity of individual voices as early as 1920. I will argue in the conclusion that this represented a

---

3   *Marx and Engels, Selected correspondence (Moscow, Foreign Languages Press, 1955) p. 503*

4   *Lenin V.I. Collected Works Vol 30 (Moscow, Progress Publishers,1965) p, 492.*

cauldron of ideas about proletarian poetics yet to be superseded. I find support in perceiving a link between the Chartists and the October Revolution in the early work of Reg Groves.[5] Also later with the investigations of Mark Krantz.[6] Thomas Cooper was an autodidact, embraced 'physical force Chartism', was imprisoned for his role in the General Strike of 1842, wrote the *Purgatory of Suicides: A Prison-Rhyme* in 922 Spenserian stanzas, became a 'moral force Chartist' remaining sceptical of Christianity, and eventually became an itinerant Baptist preacher denying Darwinism on biblical grounds. We can see how the laws of Historical Materialism were working here i.e. a material base for the superstructure of ideas. I will elaborate further on this, but it will be made clear that is not a mechanistic relationship if only because the dialectic is buried in history, obscured by the veil of ideology, creating its opposite. The Chartist movement was not a homogeneous one. It was fraught with divisions and factions. The major being class: 'a working-class movement with middle-class adherents.'[7] Therefore, Ernest Jones came from an aristocratic background initially joining the Chartists in 1846, he would experience imprisonment after the 'Left Turn' of 1848 writing poetry in his own blood after being denied writing materials.

So why is Chartist poetics important today? Because there is renewed interest in marginalised writing, and it is pertinent for us as we live in a profoundly divided society. A difference being there was a high level of class struggle and working people wrote as the tide of struggle ebbed and flowed during the Chartist milieu. It, also, deserves re- examination in the light of E.P. Thompson *The Making of the English Working Class (1968)* and Martha Vicinus *The Industrial Muse* (1974) both early and significant investigations.

---

5   *Groves, Reg But we shall rise again: A narrative history of Chartism (London, Secker and Warburg, 1938)*

6   *Krantz, Mark The 1842 General Strike (London, Bookmarks,2014).*

7   *Charlton, John The Chartists: The First National Workers' Movement (London: Pluto Press, 1997), p. 64.*

This 'hidden history' is again stimulating interest in academia with new publications like Anne Janowitz *Lyric and Labour in the Romantic Tradition* (1998), Mike Sanders *The Poetry of Chartism: Aesthetics, Politics, History* (2009), *Class and the Canon: Constructing Labouring Class Poetry and Poetics* (ed) Kirstie Blair and Mina Gorji (2013), and Margaret A. Loose *The Chartist Imaginary: Literary Forms in Working-Class Political Theory and Debate* (2014). I would like to stress that Chartist poetry in its first generation was largely, when committed to paper, published in a nationwide network of periodicals, journals and broadsheets. This analysis will examine a number across a socio-cultural spectrum during the period 1836-52 and refer to a second generation which were published in book form in the later nineteenth-century to the early twentieth century. The book history will be explored as my study is developed. It is important to recognize that Chartist poetics was the pinnacle of a radical autodidactic culture in Britain. It was multisource, but hunger was significant as by 'the hungry- forties' a stratum of the poor was facing starvation. I note that Thomas Frost who was a utopian socialist or Owenite but would not cross the line to fully fledged communist but was a Chartist, remembered:

We became acquainted that evening, and, in the course of many subsequent years, I passed an agreeable half-hour in the shoemaker's garret, talking by turns of politics and poetry.[8]

As my research has unfolded it became evident that this was by no means an unusual experience as a politicized working-class became increasingly interested in articulating themselves in poetic terms. It was a movement that would move leftwards.

---

8   Frost, *Thomas Forty Years' Recollections: Literary and Political (London: S. Low, Marston, Searle, and Rivington, 1880) p, 34.*

My variant of Marxist methodology is derived from György Lukács' study into the nature of Marxist dialectics. I required a rigorous theory for this investigation into Chartist poetics:

> *Let us assume for the sake of argument that recent research had disproved once and for all every one of Marx's individual theses... Orthodox Marxism, therefore, does not imply the uncritical acceptance of the results of Marx's investigations. It is not the 'belief' in this or that thesis, nor the exegesis of a 'sacred' book. On the contrary, orthodoxy refers exclusively to method.*[9]

Therefore, I am interested in Dialectical Materialism as a *method*. Firstly, the transformation from a quantitative to a qualitative condition, thus producing a new state and secondly, interdependent material opposites which are by nature antagonistic, finally 'the negation of the negation' which creates a new thesis afresh with elements of the old but also completely new material. I will delineate two core concepts: 1) the Marxist dialectic [Karl Marx never used the term dialectical materialism]. Here is Engels famous summary in *Dialectics of Nature*:

> *II. Dialectics*
>
> *(The general nature of dialectics to be developed ...in contrast to metaphysics.)*

It is, therefore, from the history of nature and human society that the laws of dialectics are abstracted. For they are nothing but the most general laws of these two aspects of historical development, as well as of thought itself. And indeed, they can be reduced in the main to three:

---

9   *Lukacs, Georg History & Class Consciousness: Studies in Marxist Dialectics (Pontypool, The Merlin Press 2010) p.1*

The law of the transformation of quantity into quality and *vice versa*;

> *The law of the interpenetration of opposites;*
>
> *The law of the negation of the negation.*
>
> *All three are developed by Hegel in his idealist fashion as mere laws of thought... The mistake... is made out to be arranged in accordance with a system of thought which itself is only the product of a definite stage of evolution of human thought. If we turn the thing round...it is clear as noonday.* [10]

Hence, we can comprehend not an abstract or Idealist dialectic but rather one grounded in material reality. Its twin, Historical Materialism, eloquently described by Karl Marx:

> *The first premise of all human history is, of course, the existence of living human individuals. Thus, the first fact to be established is the physical organisation of these individuals and their consequent relation to the rest of nature... The writing of history must always set out from these natural bases and their modification in the course of history through the action of men...*[11]

Several Marxist theoreticians and others will provide a structure of secondary scholarship. I will examine contemporary scholars of my subject with a special interest in the work of Janowitz (1998) and Sanders (2008). My argument is not that Chartist literature was superior or inferior to the bourgeois writers of the time. Rather they were the products of dialectically opposed classes cast in different objective material conditions. Thus, the poetry would be different. I shall, however, suggest that although there was a continuity with Romantic poetry especially during

---

10   *Engels, Frederick Dialectics of Nature (Moscow, Progress Publishers, 1976) P. 62-3*

11   *Marx and Engels (1982). p.42.*

early Chartism with publications like *The Chartist Circular* which I will reflect upon in the second chapter. This diminished with the bitter General Strike of 1842 and proletarian poetry took a new turn towards didactic realism. We will then understand a leftwards move in Chartism inspired, largely, by the revolutions on continental Europe of 1848. The Programme around this tendency was simply called 'the Charter and something more.' I will illustrate a continuity of Marxist involvement in the form of poetry, publishing and politics from 1843 with the entry of Frederick Engels and continuing into the First, Second, Third and Fourth Internationals [with its splintering] in Britain through to the present day. As Bertolt Brecht suggested 'art is not a mirror to reflect reality, but a hammer to change it'[12]. Indeed, what other use would a proletarian have of it as they are the 'universal class':

> *...a class with radical chains, which cannot emancipate itself without emancipating itself from all other spheres of society and thereby emancipating all other spheres of society, which, in a word, is the complete loss of man and hence can win itself only through the complete rewinning of man*[13]

The class who must because of historical *necessity* create communism.

---

12   Brecht, Bertolt in Paulo Freire: A Critical Encounter (1993) by Peter McLaren and Peter Leonard, p. 80."

13   Marx and Engels, Collected Works, iii, p. 186, 50 vols published or in preparation (London, 1975-).

1.

The Romantic Experience In Relation To The Chartist Poetic.

This chapter will examine some of the abstractions that lie behind the modern debates around the relationship of Romantic poetry to a working-class Chartist poetics. To arrive at an understanding, we need to examine the most current thinkers and then place them in a narrative of literary theory. This will be the main purpose of this chapter; theorising and positioning. Firstly, Mike Sanders in his recent exploration of Chartism argues: 'Indeed, it is necessary to return to the work of this neglected 1930's critic, Christopher Caudwell, to begin to comprehend the political effect of poetry'[14]. Sanders quotes Caudwell: 'a poem's content is not just emotion, it is organised emotion, an organised emotional attitude to a piece of external reality.'[15] I continue along a similar line as Mike Sanders in perceiving cogency in some of the positions of Christopher Caudwell:

> [The] contradiction between individual man or natural man, and associated or civilized man, is what makes poetry necessary, and gives it its meaning and its truth. Poetry is a production or economic activity of man. To separate it from its foundation makes its development impossible to understand.[18]

We understand that for Christopher Caudwell poetry was as essential to humanity as 'labour'. It was an aspect of what Karl Marx had called our essence or 'species-being'. Although I

14   Sanders, Mike *The Poetry of Chartism: Aesthetics, Politics, History* (Cambridge, Cambridge University Press, 2009). Kindle, 439.

15   Caudwell, Christopher, *Illusion and Reality* (Lawrence & Wishart, 1973 [1937], p34-40
18 Caudwell, Christopher *Culture as Politics* (Pluto, London, 2018). p 79

recognise the problematic nature of the association between the economic base and cultural superstructure. Louis Althusser in *Lenin on Philosophy and other Essays* is interesting here when he claimed art can illuminate aspects of the everyday 'sensuous activity' (Marx) of man in the material world. He used the example of Alexandr Solzhenitsyn who had employed literature to illustrate the 'cult of personality' in Stalinist Russia. However, he believed only scientific knowledge can provide the capacity to change it (Althusser, 2010 pp.153-155). He argued art 'in the language of Spinoza it puts the conclusions before the premises.' (Althusser 2010 p. 153).

Secondly, Anne Janowitz (1998) in her significant and contemporaneous study argued that a dialectic of 'Romantic lyricism' and a 'collective embodied experience of plebeian verse' found fulfilment in the writing of William Morris.[16] She seeks to create a dialectic between the solitary voice associated with Romanticism and the concomitant collective voice of the people. Anne Janowitz understands that there are two component parts in the development from Romantic to Chartist poetry and beyond, a dialectic. The two-component parts are firstly a position which relies on the rejection of theoreticians like John Stuart Mill's definition of Romanticism as a self-sufficient 'lyric' in 1833. Anne Janowitz quotes him: 'feeling confessing itself, in moments of solitude.'[17] She rebuffs in a similar vein, Harold Bloom: 'the sovereignty of the solitary soul… the deep self, our ultimate inwardness.'[18] She argued that both those critics have contributed to the dominant discourse which has shaped

Romantic poetry and does indeed constitute a view of the 'Lyric-I' by which she meant the concept of the Romantic poet

---

16   Janowitz, Anne *Lyric and Labour in the Romantic tradition*, (Cambridge, Cambridge University Press, (1998), p.7

17   Mill, John Stuart. *"Thoughts on Poetry and Its Varieties." The Crayon*, vol. 7, no. 4, 1860, pp. 93

18   *ww.jstor.org/stable/25528035. Cambridge University Press, (1998), p.7*

as a solitary voice. We understand Anne Janowitz maintained this position in her argument to provide the thesis to be contradicted by her antithesis, the second component part. This is a 'transpersonal Lyric':

> *This is a lyricism of sociality, of transpersonality rather than transcendence, of achieving connections, and one which, embodying a poetic structure of argument between individualism and communitarianism is both an imagined site for the self-development and imagined instantiation of selves. So, the study aims to understand the position of a communitarian lyric in the tradition of romanticism.*[19]

Janowitz states she will give priority to this communitarian aspect of Romanticism. However, although this sounds persuasive, exactly how does one achieve the conditions where the Chartist poets Thomas Cooper and Ernest Jones, who she foregrounds, would have been able to create a collective proletarian poetic. As opposed to one which disintegrated with the failure of the Chartist movement to achieve the demands of Left Chartism's 'the Charter and something more.' Her weakness is that her research fails to explore the momentous events for international proletarian literature of the October Revolution. So, she depends on Anglo-Communism rather than proletarian internationalism in the last instance. Although Janowitz alludes to the Chartist mass movement as a precursor to the Paris Commune[20]. I reiterate my position is that the masses must hold State power in order to facilitate the triumph of their poetics. The highest point of labouring- class poetics occurred before the Stalinist counter-revolution in the USSR i.e. between 1917-29 and its defeat was solidified at the Writers Congress in 1934.

---

19   *Janowitz (1998) pp.7-8 Janowitz (1998), p.8.*

20   *See Janowitz, Anne (1998) pp228-230 for a discussion of British socialists and the Paris Commune.*

Nevertheless, her work is important to the first chapter of this dissertation because she correctly illustrates that E. P Thompson's work was flawed when he argued that William Blake was the last poet who threaded together the discourses of artisan radicalism and romanticism.[21] However because she argues that Chartist poetry as 'at home in both cultures' we thus differ on the potential for and on the nature of proletarian poetry. Janowitz remains a Morrisist 'Pilgrim of Hope'. So, my discontent with Janowitz's material is that she finds the fruition of proletarian poetic in William Morris and beyond that although only in writing like that around C.N.D. provided glimmers of hope. Again, paradoxically, she argues W. H. Auden's 'Spain' 'was his greatest poem in the communitarian tradition of Romanticism.' (Janowitz, 1998, p. 234). She unfortunately drifts into the position, of to use Boris Arvatov comment on Morris, that of 'a petty-bourgeois socialist', one caught between the two great contending classes of capitalism.

In order to provide a provisional framework for this debate I will examine Ernest Jones poem *The Factory Town* from three perspectives: 1) my reading, 2) Janowitz's and, 3) Margret A. Loose's.

The Factory Town.

The night had sunk along the city,
It was a bleak and cheerless hour;
The wild-winds sung their solemn ditty
To cold, grey wall and blackened tower.
The factories gave forth lurid fires
From pent-up hells within their breast;
Even Ætna's burning wrath expires
But man's volcanoes never rest.

---

21   See Thompson, E.P, *The Making of the English Working Classes* (Harmondsworth, Penguin, 1965), p915

Women, children, men were in,
Locked in dungeons close and black,
Round the wheel, the modern rack!
E'en the very stars seemed troubled
With the mingled fume and roar;
The city like a cauldron bubbled,[22]

Ernest Jones employed a ballad form for *The Factory Town* and Janowitz speculates that because of its length the poem was sung. I agree as the tradition of the street balladeers were common currently and of course hymn singing in the dissenting tradition. This couplet is Ernest Jones at his best. It is not tendentious writing, but he is employing poetry to not only agitate but raise-consciousness about the question of urbanization, the industrial revolution and the emergence of an industrial proletariat:

The wild-winds sung their solemn ditty
To cold, grey wall and blackened tower.

The addressee hears the 'wild winds' with both alliteration and assonance [tools employed to some effect by Jones.] They in fact 'sing' a 'solemn ditty. Then he uses enjambment to suddenly increase the pace and then bring to an abrupt halt with a caesura followed by hitting a wall with the harsh 'b' of blackened tower. Anne Janowitz calls this poem: 'One of Jones 'most striking in *The Labourer.*' (Janowitz, 1998, p181). Here her reading is sound and persuasive about 'double alienation'. 'The labourers labour is separated from him and reified from him and reified into the made products. And then again as he himself is reified and deprived of his self-identity' (Janowitz, 1998 pp181-183). Here she is relying, correctly in my view, on the young Marx. A method I also use in this dissertation.

---

22   *Ernest Jones The Labourer.*

> *Yet the master proudly shows*
> *To foreign stranger's factory scenes:*
> *'These are the men – and engines these –*
> *'I see nothing but machines!'*[23]

Margret A. Loose's reading has merit. She takes the 'wild winds' I alluded to and contrasts them with 'spitting seas' [L 2-3, 86] and perceives them as metaphors 'for the coming war between workers and masters' (Loose, A. Margaret, 2014, p. 26). Although, I would argue it is not as integrated into the theoretical issues of the day as Janowitz's.

I argue that Wordsworth's early poetry had its foundation in the collapse of community which Wordsworth laments in his letter January 4th, 1804 to Charles Fox in which he sent the 2nd edition of *Lyrical Ballads* and made special reference to 'The Brothers' and 'Michael'. Both examples of a culture in decline as the industrial revolution transformed Britain[24]. Romanticism could be understood as having gestated in a political tradition which achieved its highest point in France with a revolution which would shake the continent in 1789. Jean-Jacques Rousseau had claimed in *The Social Contract (1762)*:'Man is born free, and everywhere he lives in chains.'[25] It is often presumed that in Britain the ramifications of this politico-cultural tidal wave was limited to a group of emerging bourgeois or disaffected members of the aristocracy such as William Wordsworth and Lord Byron respectively. Artists, poets, and intellectuals would have commented on these momentous events like Edmund Burke. But what of the mass of people who created history. Were they silent? Until recently the 'big six' had dominated the discourse: William Blake, William Wordsworth, Samuel-Taylor Coleridge,

---

23   *Janowitz (1998) p, 182.*

24   *Wordsworth, William Letters of William Wordsworth: a new selection [ed] Alan G. Hill. (Oxford, Oxford University Press, 1984) pp. 40-45.*

25   *Rousseau, Jean-Jacques. On the Social Contract (New York, Dover Thrift Editions, 2016) p. 1.*

John Keats, Percy Bysshe Shelley and Lord Byron. Because of the scholarship which originated in the work of Raymond Williams which matured into Cultural Materialism and contemporary studies like Duncan Wu *Romanticism* (1994) followed by Duncan Wu *Romantic Women Poets (1997) and* the terrain had been broadened. However, it was not until the publication of John Goodridge [Ed] *Nineteenth Century English Labouring Poets in Three Volumes*, (2006) that scholars had a substantial pool of working-class poetry which did not originate in the previous USSR (Kovalev, 1956). As I shall illustrate in the next chapter (Kovalev, 1956) had established an early orthodoxy in the field of Chartist literature.

I will employ William Wordsworth in this chapter as a barometer of the epoch. Largely because he lived through the entirety of it unlike any of the other major poets from the ruling elite. Anne Janowitz understands his work over time as 'Jacobinism-in-recoil' (Janowitz 2008, p. 40) which is a phrase she borrowed from E.P. Thompson to describe Wordsworth's apparent retreat from the revolutionary cause. He had been in France when the people confronted their oppressors. It is significant that the only part of *The Prelude* to be published in Wordsworth's lifetime was the famous pro-revolutionary extract from Book X claimed James. K Chandler[26].

> *'O pleasant exercise of hope and joy!*
> *For mighty were the auxiliaries which then stood*
> *Upon our side, us who were strong in love!*
> *Bliss was it in that dawn to be alive,*
> *But to be young was very Heaven! O times,*
> *In which the meagre, stale, forbidding ways*
> *Of custom, law, and statute, took at once*
> *The attraction of a country in romance!*

---

26   *See Chandler, James K Wordsworth's Second Nature: A Study in the Poetry and Politics (Chicago, University of Chicago Press, 1984) p 46-7.*

When Reason seemed the most to assert her
rights When most intent on making of herself
A prime enchantress—to assist the work,
Which then was going forward in her name![27].

It will be argued that a radical British working-class tendency was impacted upon by the political and cultural effects of the French revolution. Although there was a Jacobean moment in Britain it took a far more advanced form in Ireland with an organized insurrection by the United Irishmen in 1798 which was brutally and bloodily suppressed on the orders of Lord Castlereagh. He would also be responsible for the Peterloo Massacre outside of Manchester in 1819. Shelley felt driven to write *The Mask of Anarchy* after the bloodletting in Manchester:

As I lay asleep in Italy
There came a voice from over the Sea,
And with great power it forth led me
To walk in the visions of Poesy.
I met Murder on the way-
He had a mask like
Castlereagh-
Very smooth he looked,
yet grim;
Seven blood-hounds followed him:
All were fat; and well they might
Be in admirable plight, And d two by two,
He tossed the human hearts to chew
Which from his wide cloak he drew[28]

Lord Byron's assaults on Castlereagh were if anything, more belligerent and bellicose than Shelley's denunciation of the

27   *Wordswoth, William The Major Works (Oxford, Oxford University Press, 2000) p.548-550.*

28   *Shelley, Percy Bysshe, The Major Works (Oxford, Oxford University Press, 2003) p.400.*

massacre at Peterloo, an early suffrage gathering. Byron used both cutting satire and something boarding on 'hatred' of colonial oppression as he scribed these lines about the Irish Uprising of 1798 and its consequences in *The 'Dedication to Don Juan'*:

> *The intellectual eunuch Castlereagh...*
> *Cold-blooded, smooth-faced, placid miscreant*
> *Dabbling its sleek young hands in Erin's gore.*[29]

I shall illustrate in Chapter Three the importance of the colonial rule of Britain in Ireland to Chartism and its poetry. Hence, we can comprehend a pro-revolutionary propensity amongst both first and second-generation Romantic poets who had benefited from the emergent industrial complex, capitalism, in one way or another and then turned their pens against capitalism's excesses. Nevertheless, as Karl Marx speculated about Shelley, he was the only one of them who was a 'thourghgoing revolutionary and would always have belonged to the Socialist vanguard.'[30]

The case of William Wordsworth, as I argued, was intriguing. He was possibly the most read of the major Romantic poets by the bourgeoisie. As he lived throughout the period it was possible to gauge his writing against a protracted and turbulent period of working-class struggle. The French Revolution was in nature a bourgeois revolution. However, in England change was also in the air and it would spawn the London Corresponding Society, which at its height had 3,000 paid-members.[31] The Pitt government feared revolution and put the leadership on trial for High Treason for which they were acquitted. However, a defence

---

29   Byron, Lord *The Major Works (Oxford, Oxford University Press, 2008) p.375-376.*

30   Marx, Karl & Engels Frederick *Literature and Art: Selections from Their Writings (New York, International Publishers, 1947) p. 132.*

31   Hunt, Jocelyn B. *Understanding the London Corresponding Society a Balancing Act between Adversaries Thomas Paine and Edmund Burke. Thesis. University of Waterloo, 2013. pp. 1-13.*

fund was created and a 'Citizen Wordsworth' contributed 1s - 0d.[32] In *A Letter to the Bishop of Llandaff (1793)* Wordsworth echoed Thomas Paine: 'Political convulsions have been said particularly to call forth concealed abilities…'[33] See Thomas Paine, *Rights of Man, II. 420:*

> *It appears to general observation, that revolutions create genius and talents; but those events do no more than bring them forward. There is existing in man, a mass of sense lying in a dormant state.*[34]

As late as 1821 Wordsworth argued when asked by James Losh about his changed political opinions, the middle-aged poet answered:

> *If I were addressing those who have dealt so liberally with the words Renegade Apostate, etc., I should retort the charge upon them, and say, you have been deluded by Places and Persons, while I have stuck to Principles —*
>
> *I abandoned France, and her Rulers, when they abandoned the struggle for Liberty, gave themselves up to Tyranny, and endeavoured to enslave the world.*[35]

After the planting of what E.P. Thompson called 'The Liberty Tree'[36]. A metaphor for an incipient wave of proletarian class struggle in Britain, followed by the biting chill of reaction and then the rise of a new wave of hope and struggle in the guise of Chartism. Thomas Carlyle in his essay *Chartism* (1839) raised

---

32   *Pamphlet entitled London Corresponding Society, Nov 19th, 1794 (1795) p.5*

33   *Wordsworth, William. Wordsworth's Political Writings (Kindle Locations 1097-1099). Humanities-eBooks. Kindle Edition.*

34   *Wordsworth, William. Wordsworth's Political Writings (Kindle Locations 8149-8150). Humanities-eBooks. Kindle Edition*

35   *Wordsworth, W. The letters of William and Dorothy Wordsworth: The later years, 1821-1853 (2nd ed.) (Vols. 1-4). (Oxford, Oxford University Press, 1978-1988), I:*

36   *Thompson, E.P. The Making of the English Working Class (London, Penguin, 1991) p.111.*

the "Condition of England Question" I.e. mass poverty and alienation amongst the working class which he believed was caused by lassie- faire capitalism, Mammonism in the aristocracy and scientific materialism. He too feared the English proletariat would create a revolution.

However, another theoretical tendency was spreading its tentacles into its natural subject, it's world-historic subject, the proletariat. Engels was the first of the two founders of scientific socialism as opposed to utopian socialism to comment[37]. Engels would write: 'These six points harmless as they seem, are sufficient to overthrow the whole English Constitution, Queen and Lords included.'[38] This was because he understood them as transitional demands, i.e. neither stressing minor reformist or exaggerating any revolutionary potential in the context of that place and time and, therefore, able to mobilize workers to seek the contestation of state power. He understood this to be their historically necessary task. The Chartists' Six Demands which were set out in the Crown and Anchor public house on 28th February 1837 by William Lovett on behalf of The London Workingman's Association:

1. A vote for every man twenty-one years of age, of sound mind, and not undergoing punishment for a crime.

2. The secret ballot to protect the elector in the exercise of his vote.

3. No property qualification for Members of Parliament in order to allow the constituencies to return the man of their choice.

4. Payment of Members, enabling tradesmen, working men, or other persons of modest means to leave or interrupt their livelihood to attend to the interests of

---

37   *See Engels, Fredrick Socialism: Utopian or Scientific (London, Bookmarks, 1993)*

38   *Marx, Karl & Engels, Frederick Collected Works in 50 volumes, vol 4, p.518 (New York, International Publishers, 2004).*

the nation.

5. Equal constituencies, securing the same amount of representation for the same number of electors, instead of allowing less populous constituencies to have as much or more weight than larger ones.

6. Annual Parliamentary elections, thus presenting the most effectual check to bribery and intimidation, since no purse could buy a constituency under a system of universal manhood suffrage in each twelve-month period.

Leon Trotsky, who maintained the English Revolution and the Chartists laid bare the myth of English gradualism suggested that class struggle is central to the creation of art:

Generally speaking, art is an expression of man's need for a harmonious and complete life, that is to say, his need for those major benefits of which a society of classes has deprived him. That is why a protest against reality, either conscious or unconscious, active or passive, optimistic or pessimistic, always forms part of a really creative piece of work. Every new tendency in art has begun with rebellion.[39]

We would see that a new dialectic of the class would create not only something quantitatively new but a dialectical leap to a qualitatively different situation with the masses. It was a 'leap 'but also had a linear nature. An inheritance from previous working-class struggles in the form of an organised working class press for which there was a material base. Ulrich Schwab commented there was 'a demand for serious reading material amongst the workers.'[40] The response of the British state apparatus in 1815 was to try and suppress the workers' press with stamp duty. It became

---

39   *https://www.marxist.com/art-politics-our-epoch-tro sky080107*

40   *Schwab, Ulrich The poetry of the Chartist Movement: A Literary and Historical Study*

known as 'a Tax on knowledge' and several radical papers went underground. Notably, *Black Dwarf* launched by Thomas Wooler in 1817 which frequently quoted William Shakespeare[41]. Also, of note was *The Poorman's Guardian* 1831-1835 was founded by Henry Hetherington as a successor to his earlier (1830–31) penny daily *Penny Papers for the People*, as an outright challenge to authority. Published at the low price of a penny per weekly copy it bore the politically provocative heading: 'Published contrary to 'law' to try the power of 'might' against 'right"[42] Nevertheless, the working-class press was variable and certainly in periods of low class struggle was sentimental and sensationalist. Looking at the growth of a class-based literature in the nineteenth century generally, Martha Vicinus argued its "variety grew out of many long-developing political and social movements."[43]

Why did Chartism become a movement sustained by poetry? I address many of the practical questions in Chapter Two. One answer is that unlike the discourse of the 'big six' of Romanticism it was a cross-generic phenomenon. It was not disciplined by a learning based in Latin and Greek, although as Thomas Hardy later understood in *Jude the Obscure*, many workers aspired to a classical education. However, *Jude the Obscure* describes a period of low class struggle and hence the atomised worker, Nevertheless, if we briefly examine two other revolutionary moments and recall Thomas Paine and Leon Trotsky as above on revolution and art from *The Rights of Man* and *Art and Politics in Our Epoch* respectively. The analytical apparatus for an argument becomes apparent, it is when the masses and their poets rebelled. There

---

(Dordrecht: Kluwer Academic Publishers, 1987) p. 27.

41   *Prince, Katherine Shakespeare in the Early Working-Class Press pp 131-132 in [ed] Arura Krishnamurthy The Working-Class Intellectual in Eighteenth-and Nineteenth- Century Britain (London, Taylor & Francis, 2009)*

42   *http://www.bl.uk/learning/citizenship/campaign/myh/newspapers/gallery1/paper4/ poormansguardian.ht ml*

43   *Vicinus, Martha, The Industrial Muse: A Study of Nineteenth Century Working-Class Literature (London, Croom Helm, 1974), p.94.*

have always been poets as Caudwell argued they had existed as priests and shamans.

However, independently of Caudwell we can understand an insight from Walter Benjamin in *The Work of Art in the Age of Mechanical Reproduction* (2008 [1936]). He illustrates the nature of modernization on the artistic process:

> *The work of art when it can be reproduced by technological means… the technological means frees the work of art, for the first time in history, from its existence as a parasite upon ritual.*[44]

He concluded one should argue that: 'Communism's reply is to politicise art' (2008 [1936]) p. 38. We see the rise of proletarian culture. Another reason the Chartists wrote poetry was an established tradition of street ballads. In the words of Malcolm Chase:

> *Poetry mattered to the Chartists, especially after November 1839 [the defeat of the Newport uprising]. Verse, rather than the speaker's platform or journalism, was the safest public space wherein to proclaim revolutionary sentiment. To write and read (especially aloud) or sing verse was also to confront polite culture. It located Chartism within an intellectual and political tradition that extended back to the English Revolution; Milton and Marvel were amongst the most popular models for Chartist poetry.*[45]

But what of my barometer of the period in England, William Wordsworth, and the concept of 'Jacobinism-in-recoil'. I hope that I have intimated that might not have been a totally satisfactory

---

44   Benjamin, Walter *The Work of Art in the Age of Mechanical Reproduction* (London, Penguin Great Ideas, 2008 [1936]) pp. 11-12.

45   Chase. Malcolm *Chartism: A New History* (Manchester, Manchester University Press, 2007) p.118.

reading. I looked to John Williams *Wordsworth: Romantic Poetry and Revolution* (1989) who argued William Wordsworth was after all thinking consistently and this could be explained by employing the Gramscian category 'of a traditional intellectual'.

As Antonio Gramsci maintained of the 'traditional intellectual':

> *He is seeking intellectual categories which were pre-existing, and which, moreover, appeared as representatives of an historical continuity uninterrupted even by the most complicated and radical changes, of social and political forms.*[46]

This may seem a little rigid and harsh, but it reflects William Wordsworth's class orientation. He might well have sympathised, yet more, he did feel an empathy with the rural poor and toyed with revolution, but he was never going to mount the barricades. Rather Antonio Gramsci's concept of the 'organic intellectual' is of explanatory value when examining Chartist poets. He had argued:

> *That all men are intellectuals, in that all have intellectual and rational faculties, but not all men have the social function of intellectuals*[47].

So, for Gramsci working class or 'organic intellectuals' contest the ruling-class hegemony in 'a war of manoeuvre' with 'traditional intellectuals' until the time is ripe for 'social revolution'. We can understand Chartist poets as examples of 'organic intellectuals' challenging the bourgeois dominance with their material, the poetry. As here in the concluding lines of Ernest Jones' poem:

---

46   *Gramsci, Antonio 'The Formation of Intellectuals' in The Modern Prince and Other Writings (New York, International Publishers, 1978), p, 119*

47   *Gramsci, Antonio Selections from the Prison Notebooks. (London, Lawrence and Wishart, 1982) p.8.*

The Cornfield and the Factory.

The very sun shines pale on a dark earth,
Where quivering engines groan their horrid mirth,
And black smoke-offerings, crimes and curses, swell
From furnace-altars of incarnate hell!
The demon laughs, and still his arm he waves,
That thins the villages but fills the graves.
Through bleak, deserted fields he loves to roam,
Where shines the furnace on hell's harvest-home.
'Tis this has stilled the laughter of the child,
And made man's mirth less holy, but more wild!
Bade Heav'n's pure light from woman's eye depart,
And trodden love from out her gentle heart.
'Tis this, that wards the sunshine from the sod... [48]

'The Factory Town' which was in ballad form while 'The Cornfield and the Factory' was an experimental poem written later and published in a book rather than a worker's newspaper.

Ernest Jones was still a convinced socialist but his parlance and the troupes he employs had altered. The reader still comprehended a dichotomy between town and country. However, a 'demon laughs' which is a metaphor not only for industrial pollution but also his demonic effluence generally. He is spewing fire, brimstone, smoke and evil. Thus, the speaker can terrify and depopulate: 'thin the villages' and 'fill the graves. Jones uses alliteration quite convincingly 'hell's harvest home'. The addressee feels flung into the Inferno. Then the poem becomes a morality tale as man is 'made more wild' and 'Heav'n's pure light from women's eyes depart.' A very Victorian gender stereotyping. Even 'the very smile of God' as one would have expected in Hell does not penetrate. It was certainly not Dante. However, Jones is endeavouring not to use the language of current social strife in this poem. Rather

48   *Jones, Ernest The Battle-Day and Other Poems (London, Routledge & Co, 1855). p. 93-94.*

for him that period was in limbo as he had broken with Marx and Engels over the question of revolutionaries agitating in the new trade union movement. So, it is consistent that he would harness the registers of Evangelical Christianity to further his ends. Although unlike Thomas Cooper he had not eschewed his revolutionary beliefs. Indeed, he is still contesting hegemony but not with the language concomitant with a heightened period of class struggle.

2.

Contrasting Chartist Publications And Perspectives On Poetry.

An orthodoxy had been created in the first anthologies of Chartist literature. e.g. (Yuri Kovalev, 1956)[49]. It was originally used for teaching in the USSR. Then published in the West by Central Books with his analysis, in Russian, translated at Manchester University two years later. It was published later that year in the U.S.A, *Victorian Studies Vol. 2, No. 2 (December 1958)*. His argument was that Chartist poetry had almost 'mechanistically' arisen out of the period which the Victorians came to call Romanticism and then developed its own character. However, he was weak in many areas e.g. mechanistic materialism rather than dialectical materialism, a lack of weight given to John Ruskin's influence on William Morris to mention two errors. His analysis has endured, in one manifestation or another, until recently. As with all theoretical models it required readjustment and revisiting of the primary texts in the hope of devising new solutions and the possibility of opening up new areas of research. Hence a more complex narrative has now emerged. Kovalev's pioneering anthology and the question of the centrality of Romanticism to the Chartist poetic is a debate which has been reanimated in recent years. There is doubtlessly an echo of Romanticism in Chartist poetics. The question is whether they were able to make a dialectical leap into something innovatory. An autonomous literature is another question. An important area in the evaluation of labouring-class poetics is its limitations, strengths and futures.

---

49   *Kovalev, Y. An anthology of Chartist Literature (Moscow, Foreign Languages Publishing House, 1956).*

For the Chartists, literature and especially poetry were of huge significance.

As Malcolm Chase made clear 'Chartist poets aspired to a greater sophistication than the street balladeers of the time, successfully so.'[50] *The Chartist Circular (1839- 1842)* and *The Labourer (1847-1848)* espoused contradictory ideas about working- class poetry argued Sanders (Blair, K & Mina. G, [ed] 2013, p.71). I will examine that relationship but also by extension Feargus O'Connor's mighty *The Northern Star (1837-1852)* which was the literary spine of the Chartist movement. This is revealing because Feargus O'Connor was the proprietor of *The Northern Star* and co-owner and editor of *The Labourer* with Ernest Jones in 1847-8. Hence, we can comprehend how the perspectives on poetry changed over a longer period within Chartism and in more detail. Although neither Thomas Cooper nor Ernest Jones wrote for *The Chartist Circular.* Mainly lesser known and often anonymous writers did, and this will facilitate a deeper understanding of the relationship between Romanticism which was the dominant genre within *The Chartist Circular* and the earlier Chartist movement. We will perceive a shift in the aftermath of the failure of the 1842 General Strike away from a working-class adherence to Romanticism towards a harsher, poetic realism. That is, the poet was no longer seen as the genius through which poetry came into being (Wordsworth, *Introduction to Lyrical Ballads* 1802) albeit in the language of the common people or the poets 'as the unacknowledged legislators of the world.' (Shelley, *In Defence of Poetry*, 1832). The poet became the activist whom through which the oppressed will achieve a communitarian and equitable social formation. Thus, the first wave of Chartist writers would become the mouthpieces of what Thomas Cooper called 'Knowledge, the great Enfranchiser' (Randell, 1999, p.184). This suggested that the future of labouring-class poetry could be, not merely a vehicle for winning the vote, but more ambitious. One aspiration suggested

---

50   *Chase, Malcolm (2007) p.119*

by Thomas Cooper was 'a language of our own.' Meaning a distinct and articulate discourse dialectically opposed to the varied and competing narrative of poets like Elizabeth Barrett Browning, Robert Browning, Alfred Tennyson, Mathew Arnold and, at the time, marginalized writers like Christina Rossetti and later the Jesuit priest, Gerald Manley Hopkins. However, for working-class poets like the young Thomas Cooper and increasingly so with Ernest Jones didactic poetry to suit an epoch and the Chartist struggle would become the norm. Interestingly both Marx and Engels argued against a simplistic tendentious poetry and admired Shakespeare, Schiller, Byron, Shelley and Heinrich Heine who was a friend.

The Northern Star was by far the most successful of the Chartist newspapers or journals achieving a circulation of 50,000 at its peak during the Birmingham Riots in July 1839.[51] At times between 1838-52 the poetry editors were sometimes so inundated with poetry that:

> *we have received so much poetry as a donkey could draw and [are] gutted with almost as a jackass had what claims to be poetry waiting for them.*[52]

It claimed a verbal range of seven per copy being read aloud by literate workers to their illiterate comrades. This exhibited a high level of solidarity. *The Northern Star* of Leeds, a weekly, as I mentioned became the backbone of Chartism was founded by Feargus O'Connor who in 1837 had named it after the Ulster paper of the insurrectionary nationalist group the *United Irishmen*. They had risen nationally under the leadership of a Protestant Wolfe Tone and been suppressed by the British in 1798. O'Connor was imprisoned for a 'seditious libel' in 1839 written in *The Northern Star* and upon his release from York Castle Prison

---

51   Epstein, James *The Lion of Freedom* (London, Breviary Stuff Publications 2015) p.59.
52   *Northern Star, 1st January 1842.*

in 1841 *The Lion of* Freedom was first sung, composed by Thomas Cooper. Cooper was a fascinating man. He would be imprisoned in 1842 during the General Strike for inciting a riot. *The Lion of Freedom* became a very popular poetic song and was often roared wherever Feargus O'Connor appeared. Although later in his life Thomas Cooper would deny it was composed by him or so Edward Royle claimed.[53]

"The Lion of Freedom,"

'Lion of Freedom is come from his den;

We'll rally around him, again and again:
We'll crown him with laurel, our champion to be:

O'Connor the patriot: for sweet Liberty!

The pride of the people—He's noble and brave—
A terror to tyrants—a friend to the slave:
The bright star of Freedom—the noblest of men:
We'll rally around him, again and again.

Who strove for the patriots—was up night and day—
To save them from falling to tyrants a prey?
'Twas fearless O'Connor was diligent then:
We'll rally around him, again and again.

Though proud daring tyrants his body confined,
They never could conquer his generous mind:
We'll hail our caged lion, now freed from his den:
We'll rally around him, again and again.
-Thomas Cooper.[54]

---

53   *Royle, Edward Chartism (London, Longman, (1996) p.108.*
54   *Cooper, Thomas The Northern Star (1841).*

Thomas Cooper wrote of O'Connor in his autobiography: 'The popularity of this song may serve to show how firmly O'Connor was fixed in the regard of a portion of the manufacturing operatives, as the incorruptible advocate of freedom. Therefore, they immediately suspected the honesty of any local leader who did not rank himself under the banner of Feargus, the leader-in-chief.' I note the that this poetic song was used in 'performance' for rousing the spirits of the masses and Thomas Cooper described it as a 'chant'. It is in ballad form, four quatrains rhyming aabb with a pronounced anaphora "We'll rally" which one can imagine whipped-up emotion in large audiences. Thomas Cooper could read out loud from the age of three:

> *Thomas Cooper had his first encounter with Byron's poetry: in my thirteenth year, by some accident there fell into my hands one of the cantos of Childe Harold's Pilgrimage and the drama of Manfred. I had them in my hands for only a few hours, and I knew nothing of their noble author's life or reputation, but they seemed to create a new sense within me. I wanted more poetry to read from that time but could get hold of none that thrilled through my nature like Byron's. A couple of years later as an apprentice shoemaker, Cooper was introduced to the poetry of Burns by his master. As with Somerville, the effect was exhilarating – 'The pathos of Burns took possession of my whole nature almost as completely as the fire and force of Byron.* [55]

I shall undertake an analysis of 'The Poetry Column' of *The Northern Star* 1838– 1852 with the statistics published by Sanders (2009, p71). By way of an interpretation, I note Thomas Julian Harney was appointed editor in 1843 and after his ideological disagreement with Feargus O'Connor over the influence of Marx and Engels the paper moved to London in 1844. *The Northern Star* went into relative decline after the revolutions of 1848 as

---

55   *Cooper, Thomas The Life of Thomas Cooper (London, Hodder & Stoughton, 1873) p..176*

shown in the number of poems published. We can also ascertain that after the failure of the General Strike in 1842 within two years the division between 'non-Chartist produced poems' and poems written by Chartists takes approximately half each. Whereas previously the Chartist poetry was in the ascendency. This I suggest reflected the division of labour between manual and mental labour which the young Marx in 1844 had seen at the heart of human alienation that is inherent in capitalism:

> *Estranged labour not only (1) estranges nature from man and (2) man from himself, from his own function, from his vital activity; because of this it also estranges man from his own species. It turns his species-life into a means for his individual life. Firstly, it estranges species-life and individual life, and secondly, it turns the latter in its abstract form, into the purpose for the former, also in its abstract form and estranged form.*[56]

This was a breakthrough, I would argue, for the way we comprehend our species- being or essence. What Marx had done was lift the veil on why the worker feels alienated from their labour or species-being under the circumstances of early capitalism, why they felt estranged from nature and each other. William Morris after recognizing his indebtedness to John Ruskin would later advocate Socialism as the only solution to this malady:

> *Yet it may be remembered that civilisation has reduced the working man to such a skinny and pitiable existence...It is the province of art to set the true ideal of a full and reasonable life before him, a life in which the perception and creation of beauty, the enjoyment of real pleasure that is, shall be felt as necessary to man as his daily bread.*[57]

---

56   *Marx, Karl Early Writings (London, Pelican Marx Library,1977) p.328.*

57   *Morris, William Useful Work v, Useless Toil (London, Penguin Books, Great Ideas, 2008) p.93-4.*

Here, I suggest, William Morris is delineating a complex aesthetic, one that synthesises the dialectical opposites of labour and literature. This was a seminal moment for modern aesthetics as it created an organic human unity and the possibility of living without alienation. With the revolutionary wave of 1848 and the interest was again, it seemed, centred on London after rioting, the mass meeting on Kennington Green of 200,000 and the Third Petition. This was foiled by O'Connor's huge error in judgement in not marching on parliament. It created an audience for the Left though. I will examine the 'Left Turn' and its ramifications for poetry in Chapter Three.

Mike Sanders (Blair, K & Mina. G, [ed] 2013) argued the earlier Chartist publication *The Chartist Circular* had been under the influence of Romanticism. *The Chartist Circular* had maintained a position in favour of bourgeois democracy or suffrage as understood in the original *Six Point Charter* and was also in favour of the creation of a 'National Poetry.' A front page from *The Chartist Circular:* edited by William Thompson was openly class- collaborationist. It was not a newspaper in the sense *The Northern Star* and *The Labourer* were 'but an educational journal...throughout the paper's life it had a quote from the Marquis de Lafayette as its masthead: 'For a Nation to Love Liberty, it is sufficient that she knows it: and to be free, it is sufficient that she wills it.' W. Hamish Frasier points out:

> *From the start, there was an appeal to the middle classes, whom Whig governments 'had treated with contempt', and, an appeal to 'the industrial classes' who had carried the Reform Act...Only the union of our middle-class and working classes could affect to regenerate the country...*[58]

The Chartist Circular which was published in Glasgow at its peak sold 20,000 copies and had two poetry columns. The first

---

58   *Frasier. Hamish (2005) p.92*

The Politics of Poetry existed between 11th January 1839 -March 13th, 1840. This was followed by *Literary Sketches* from 11th June 1840-April 9th, 1842. During the whole period, it published around 150 poems by at least 67 poets while *The Northern Star* published around 350 poems by at least 120 poets. So, in literary terms, it was a significant publication. As Mike Sanders maintained 'it can be argued that poetry played an even more significant role in *The Chartist Circular* than it did in *The Northern Star*.' In its first comment on the nature of poetry *The Chartist Circular* noted:

> *The gentleman critics complain that the union of poetry with politics is always hurtful to the politics, and fatal to the poetry. But these great connoisseurs must be wrong, if Homer, Dante, Shakespeare, Milton, Cowper, and Burns were poets.*

('*The Politics of Poets, No. 1*', 1840, p. 170. [59]

Mike Sanders echoed Anne Janowitz's earlier scholarship linking Romanticism and Chartism which is central to my work. Sanders observed this theme in *The Chartist Circular*: 'Shelley, Byron, Wordsworth, Coleridge and the young Southey are all discussed and praised for their Republican and/or democratic tendencies.' We can also note that the early stanzas of Book 2 Thomas Cooper's *The Purgatory of Suicides* positions his poetry in a national dialogue including Shakespeare, Milton, Sydney, Byron, a 'National Bard'. I would note a dialectic here between the objective class position of the poets idealised and that of the Chartist poets who elevated them. This can be perceived as a form of estrangement in the same way as when humanity project their 'species- being' onto an external object in a similar manner as Ludwig Feuerbach had argued the 'alienated' human beings

---

59   *Class and the Canon: Constructing Labouring-Class Poetry and Poetics, 1780-1900 (2013) (p. 157).*

projected their essence onto a God in the heavens and thus lost an element of their humanity.[60]

Is it possible to create an independent working-class literature within the confines of capitalism? I argue in a similar vein to Leon Trotsky in *Class and Art* (1924) that the possibility of a pre-revolutionary proletarian class literature is small until Socialism is created. I think the forces both objective and subjective are so immense and, indeed, corrosive to the proletarian poet under capitalism. She or he is exploited, alienated and exhausted by labour. Indeed, the question of whether the Chartist workers' movement of 1836-52 was class-conscious to the extent of having metamorphosed from being what Marx described as a 'class-in-itself' into the heightened revolutionary state of being a 'class-for- itself' is one that is unresolved even amongst Marxian commentators e.g. Gareth

Steadman-Jones *Language of Class: Studies in English working-class history*

[Rethinking Chartism, 1983], pp 90-177 for a thoughtful but totally Revisionist reading and Dorothy Thompson. *The Chartists* (London, Breviary Stuff Publications, 2013) for a slightly less Revisionist reading but one that mistaken understands the Marxist theory of history as teleological rather than dialectical.

However, the literary pages *of The Labourer,* under the control of Ernest Jones, were championing the world-view of the proletariat which is, I argue, internationalist. It was, therefore, suggested that only from a future communal society could a working class or mass poetic be drawn in the pages of *The Labourer.* Two contributions by Ernest Jones from that publication illustrate that there was also meaningful and profound literary criticism being written and read in the Chartist movement:

---

60   See Feuerbach, Ludwig *The Essence of Christianity, trans George Elliot.*

There are class poets, the same as we have class-legislators. They seize some topic interesting only to the privileged few, or, more frequently, dwell on morbid, abstract theories, that never can claim, nor even deserve general attention.

Ernest Jones, 1847a, p. 284.[61]

And:

[Chartist] poetry is, indeed the freshest and most stirring of the age; as in England, thus in France, America, Ireland, and Germany, the poetic spirit has struck the chords of liberty, and the fresh vigour of its production's contrasts proudly with the emasculated verses of a fashionable school. Yet, for many, we have expected more. What is Robert Browning doing? He, who could fire the soul of a Luria, and develop the characters of a Victor and a Charles, – he, who could depict nature's nobility in a Colombe, – has he nothing to say for popular rights? Let him eschew his kings and queens, – let him quit the pageantry of courts – and ascend into the cottage of the poor. Can Tennyson do no more than troll a courtly lay? His oak could tell other tales besides a love story.

Ernest Jones, 1847b, pp. 95–6.[62]

We understand a clear aesthetic judgement made by a man who had been a lawyer and had originated from an aristocratic background. I postulate that he would have probably had a knowledge of Kantian aesthetics and ideas of literary taste. He would certainly have been aware of John Keats *Ode to a Grecian Urn* from his pre-Chartist period:

> *When old age shall this generation waste*
> *Thou shalt remain, in midst of other woe*

---

61   Jones, Ernest (1847a) 'Review: T. Powell', The Labourer, 1:6, 284.

62   Ernest Jones The Labourer

> *Than ours, a friend to man, to whom thou sayst,*
> *"Beauty is truth, truth beauty," – that is all*
> *Ye know on earth, and all ye need to know.*
> *(lines 46–50)*[63]

What we are really looking at here is the beginning of the formation of Nations and simultaneously canonizing of English poetry and prose. As Terry Eagleton argued:

> *It is no accident that the period we are discussing [the second half of the eighteenth century, leading into the Romantic period] sees the rise of modern 'aesthetics'. … It is mainly from this era, in the work of Kant, Hegel, Schiller, Coleridge and others, that we inherit our contemporary ideas of … 'aesthetic experience', of 'aesthetic harmony' and the unique nature of the artefact... Now, this concrete, historically variable practices were being subsumed into some special, mysterious faculty known as the 'aesthetic'…. Art was extricated from the material practices, social relations and ideological meanings in which it is always caught up and raised to the status of a solitary fetish.*[64]

The endurance of beauty is a powerful metaphor in Keats' 1819 'Ode to a Grecian Urn' and would have impacted on the pre-Chartist reading of Ernest Jones. But when the knock is hard on the door of History there is a sharpening of class divisions and class- consciousness. By 1843 Engels and then Marx was intensely involved in the Chartist movement and their thinking about literature would have been an influence on Ernest Jones. Indeed, Marx in his analysis of the European revolutions of 1848 concluded: 'The social revolution cannot take its poetry from the past, only the future.' Nevertheless, the process of incipient 'canon-building' with the rise of the bourgeois nation-state and its

---

63   *Keats, John, The Complete Poems (London, Penguin Classics, 1973) p345-46.*

64   *Eagleton, Terry Literary Theory: An Introduction (Oxford, Blackwell, 1996) pp 18-19.*

consolidation were both factors, I suggest, in the marginalisation of labouring-class poetry.

Indeed, in making it a 'hidden history.'

In Britain, the poetry of Chartism was by the dawn of the European revolutions taking a harsher tone as here in Ernest Jones poem about those who betray their class. Here we perceive an upper class or professional poet who is aligned with the Chartists using onomatopoeia to convey the sense of the proletariat 'policing' their own communities. This is a phenomenon which occurred in working- class communities during periods of high 'class consciousness' or when power was contested between the proletariat and bourgeoisie e.g., 'dual power' in Russia between February and October 1917 or Catalonia during the Spanish Civil War in 1937 when there was a revolution within a civil war. Equally, at a lower level during the Miners' Strike of 1984-85 in British pit villages. Here in *The Labourer*, Vol 2, 1848 and I note that this poem is almost excluded from two recent 'polite' studies of Ernest Jones. Only a cursory remark is made by Miles Taylor[65]. It is completely ignored by Simon Rennie. [66]

THE SONG OF THE GAGGERS.

Gag—gag—gag!
Is the cry of the traitor band,
While they try, with a printed rag,
To ride like a midnight hag
On the breast of a sleeping land.

Come—knave and villain, informer and spy,
To the government mint, where you coin a lie!

65   Taylor, Miles *Ernest Jones, Chartism and the Romance of Politics 1819-1869* (Oxford, Oxford University Press, 2003) p.112.

66   Rennie, Simon *The Poetry of Ernest Jones: Myth, Song and the 'Mighty Mind'* (Routledge, London, 2016).

Gold—gold—gold!
Is the pay for the ready slave,
Whose word at a breath can destroy the bold,
In the halls where justice is bought and sold,
And the withering glance falls keen and cold
On the heart of the true and brave.

Gag—gag—gag!
Is the cry of the traitor band
While they try, with a printed rag,
To ride like a midnight hag
On the breast of a sleeping land.

We'll stay the stream in its fullest force,
We'll stop the world in its onward course—
Gag—gag—gag!
The voice of six thousand years
Shall begin at our bidding to fail and flag
Not a lip shall breathe, not a tongue shall wag
And history's page be an idle brag,
Compared to Russell's fears.

Gag—gag—gag!
Is the cry of the traitor band,
While they seek with a printed rag,
To ride like a midnight hag,
On the breast of a sleeping land.
In vain shall the blood of an Emmett have flowed,
In vain shall the breast of a miser have glowed!
Gag—Gag—Gag!
The thought in the teeming brain!
The pulse in the heart of the world shall lag,
And nations the burden of misery drag,

And Lilliput trample on Brobdingnag.
As long as a Russell shall reign.
- Ernest Jones.[67]

The refrain repeated is four times with trimeter of choking 'heavy' or strong poetic 'feet' as the speaker hands out class justice to the class traitor. This rather predictably changes from Gag-gag-gag to Gold-gold-gold/Is the pay for the ready slave. However, the alliterative 'g' sounds do sustain an atmosphere of threat. Of note, because Feargus O'Connor was the proprietor and co-editor of *The Labourer,* is Ernest Jones couplet where he links class treachery to internationalism with the Jonathon Swift allusion. *Gulliver's Travels* was written in Ireland. This is important because Ernest Jones was moving rapidly Leftwards and adopting an internationalist proletarian worldview. Therefore, he was involved with an organization called the Fraternal Democrats who were founded at a meeting held in London on September 22th, 1845. The society embraced representatives of Left Chartists and emigres with which Marx and Engels were closely involved and it was the precursor to the First International eventually created with the assistance of Marx and Engels in 1864. We understand an echo of both Byron's and Shelley's support for the anti-imperialist struggles and those of the poor. Also contrast the literary allusions in Ernest Jones poem to Swift's

Gulliver's Travels, complex satire, in comparison with Thomas Coopers' more popular *The Lion of Freedom.* The poem had earned Cooper the title 'the Chartist Laurette' together with his *The Purgatory of Suicides: A Prison-Rhyme* (1845). It was a political epic of 922 Spenserian stanzas. By 1846, he had broken with O'Connor and became a 'moral force' Chartist. The latter was very different from his earlier poetry and illustrates an attempted shift in Thomas Cooper from working-class autodidact to rise to the level of a middle-class professional poet. He was the model

---

67   *Jones, The Labourer, 1846*

for the central character in Charles Kingsley's Industrial Novel *Alton Locke* (1850).

Although the tensions between Ernest Jones and Feargus O'Connor were not fraught at that time argued Glenn Aire who commented: '*The Labourer* more so than even *The Northern Star* was a palpably O'Connoirite journal.[68] However, there is documentary evidence that suggests the two men were not so aligned ideologically. I can illustrate that Ernest Jones gravitated towards Chartism in late 1845. 'In the winter of 1845, having accidentally seen a copy of the Northern Star, and finding the political principles advocated harmonized with my own, I sought the executive and joined the Chartist movement.'[69] This made it inevitable he would meet George Harney who Paul Foot showed was a worker and an autodidact. His radical agitation could be traced all the way back to the 'Stamp Wars', the struggle for a worker's press.[70] George Harney recorded his first meeting with Engels in 1843.'It was in 1843 that he came over from Bradford from Leeds and enquired for me at *The Northern Star* office... He told me he was a constant reader of *The Northern Star* and took a keen interest in the Chartist movement. Thus, began our friendship over fifty years ago.[71] John Saville in his definitive Marxist study of Ernest Jones is absolutely clear, Marx and Jones met in November 1847.[72] Thus, it is difficult to deny the persuasiveness of V. I. Lenin's position when he argued the Chartist movement was at least from 1843 onwards 'the first genuinely mass revolutionary movement' and 'the word but one before Marxism'.

---

68   *Airey, Glenn Feargus O'Connor, Ernest Jones and The Labourer in [ed] Allen, Joan and Ashton. An Owen Papers for The People A Study of the Chartist Press (London, The Merlin Press, 2005) p.120*

69   *Saville, John Ernest Jones Chartist (London, Lawrence & Wishart, 1952) p.17.*

70   *Foot, Paul, The Vote (London, Bookmarks, 2012). pp. 89-90.*

71   *Reminiscences of Marx and Engels (Moscow, Foreign Languages Publishing House, 1963). p.192.*

72   *Saville, John (1952). p, 27.*

That is not to argue there were no other factions; variants on 'moral force' Chartism. Decent people who believed the working class needed only education and the vote alone to acquire State power. However, the extremely wealthy and their cohorts in the state apparatus will not give up power to another class unless compelled too. It is clear following the most recent scholarship i.e., Sanders, Janowitz and Margaret A. Loose that the role of poetry in the Chartist movement was ideological so people were not being introspective. There would have been time for that if they had created a new Commonwealth or, equally, The New Jerusalem, Socialism but they failed. This failure and its consequences for a British working-class poetic will be addressed in the next chapter. I have illustrated that poetry and literary criticism were prevalent in the Chartist press. I had shown a drift to the Marxist 'Left' from an explicitly class collaborationist journal through to one that published the first English edition of Marx & Engels *Communist Manifesto*. We saw how dialectical conflict is at the heart of History and how writing reflected these conflicts. I have made a case for the simultaneous rise of the modern bourgeoisie in Britain and the incipient process of creating a literary Canon. This was captured in 1872 by Mathew Arnold: "Culture, the acquainting ourselves with the best that has been known and said in the and thus with the history of the human spirit."[73] This has inevitably left 'hidden histories' for scholars to explore.

---

73   *Arnold, Mathew Literature and Dogma preface. https://hdl.handle.net/2027/ uiug.30112073726298*

3

1848, The 'Left Turn' And The Poetry Of Class Struggle.

This chapter will examine the 'Left Turn' in Chartism which had two causal factors. The first was the eruptions of revolution across continental Europe in 1848 which reinvigorated the Chartist movement. Secondly, this was compacted into a short period of intense activity after the tactical error of Feargus O'Connor of not marching on Parliament with the Third Petition after a mass meeting on Kennington Green. It was delivered by hansom cabs instead and ignored. The state sensing weakness struck. This was relatively rapidly accompanied by Left papers coming to dominance edited as follows in London: *The Democratic Review* 1849-50, [ed] George Harney, T*he Red Republican & The Friend of The People 1850-51*[ed] George Harney which contained in three editions the first English publication of Karl Marx and Frederick Engels *The Communist Manifesto* and *Notes to the People 1851-2* [ed] Ernest Jones. *The Communist Manifesto* was translated by the Marxist- Feminist Helen Macfarlane. [74] Thomas Cooper, by this time, had become a deviationist moving rapidly rightwards embracing 'moral-force' Chartism. I shall employ primary texts of poetry from a 'Left' journal and Mathew Arnold. Also see continuity with Marxian socialism, beginning in 1843 with Engels and continuing with the shift toward internationalism in the circumstances of post-1848 Chartism, through the creation of the First International until the present. Thus, agreed with the orientation of Mark O'Brien's revolutionary socialist analysis.[75]

---

74   Black, David *Helen Macfarlane (New York, Lexington Books, 2004).*

75   O'Brien, Mark *'Perish the Privileged Orders', A Socialist History of The Chartist Movement, (London, Redwords, 1995.)*

I shall employ a contrast to illustrate the polarized nature of society and thought when the adornments of ideology are torn away. Although there are graduations when that 'knock on the door' of history I mentioned earlier finally comes there are only two camps: exploiter and exploited. This will be illustrated by way of a poem written by Mathew Arnold: 'Dover Beach' and Leon Trotsky's meditation on Chartism. Firstly, Trotsky summing-up the Chartist experience:

> *The period of Chartism is immortal because over the course of its existence it affords us an abbreviated and systematic view of virtually the entire course of proletarian struggle...*[76].

Now in contrast let us examine Arnold's 'Dover Beach':

> *...the world, which seems*
> *To lie before us like a land of dreams,*
> *So various, so beautiful, so new,*
> *Hath really neither joy, nor love, nor light,*
> *Nor certitude, nor peace, nor help for pain;*
> *And we are here as on a darkling plain,*
> *Swept with confused alarms of struggle and flight,*
> *Where ignorant armies clash by night.*[77]

We see contrasting Weltanschauung or 'world-views. One, Marxian which understands the inevitability and progressive nature of 'proletarian struggle' and sees it ultimately leading to a new dialectical leap, 'the negation of the negation' and a higher level of socio-cultural development. The other comprehends a bourgeois 'new' world i.e. the establishment of capitalism as the dominant social system. However, Arnold's addressee is left in doubt as the 'speaker ejaculates three 'end-rhymes' 'pain'/

---

76   *Trotsky, Leon, Leon Trotsky on Britain (New York, Pathfinder, 2012), p. 151.*

77   *Daniel Karlin. [Ed] The Penguin Book of Victorian Verse (Penguin Classics) (p. 381). Penguin Books Ltd. Kindle Edition.*

'flight'/ 'night'. The masses are as always from the pens of rightist bourgeois commentators quite simply 'ignorant'. But whom are these 'ignorant armies'? Are they England and France as Francis O'Gorman suggested[78]?

Of course, as Arnold's speaker concurs. Or rather is Arnold alluding in the final line of the poem to the 'armies that clash by night', maybe within, the class armies. For as O'Gorman observes: 'the generalist terms of 'Dover Beach' refuses to ground itself exactly.' (O'Gorman, 2017, p.312). Ostensibly about a crisis of faith, it was probably drafted, as (O'Gorman 2017 p.312), makes clear in 1851 but was not published until 1867.

Yet in another world this was also published in 1851_in *The Red Republican & the Friend of the People*. {Ed] Julian Harney.[79] It included Ernest Jones' 'prison poems or 'Sacred Hymns' [80].

BY ERNEST JONES.

(Written in the blood of their author, whilst incarcerated in Tothill-fields' Prison.)

No. 1. —HYMN FOR ASCENSION DAY.

Chorus.

Freedom is risen!
Freedom is risen!
Freedom is risen to-day!

78   Francis O'Gorman *Victorian Poetry: The Annotated Edition (Oxford, Blackwell, 2017)* p.312.

79   *Harney, G. Julian The Red Republican & the Friend of the People. London: Merlin Press* [etc.], *https://catalog.hathitrust.org/Record/012289057*

80   *https://catalog.hathitrust.org/Record/012289057 p.37.*

Single voice.

She burst from prison,
She burst from prison,
She broke from her
gaolers away!

Chorus.

When was she born?
How was she nurst
Where was her cradle laid?

Single voice.

In want and scorn;
Reviled and curst;
'Mid the ranks of
toil and trade.

Chorus.

And hath she gone
On her Holy morn,
Nor staid for the
long work-day?

Single voice.

From heaven she came,
On earth to remain,
And bide with her
sons alway.

Chorus.

Did she break the grave,
Our souls to save,
And leave our bodies in hell?

Single voice.

To save us alive,
If we will but strive,
Body and soul as well.

Chorus.

Then what must we do
To prove us true?
And what is the
law she gave?

                Single voice.   *Never fulfil*
                                                      A tyrant's will,
                                                   Nor willingly live a slave.

                Chorus.   *Then this we'll do,*
                                                      To prove us true,
                                                And follow the law she gave:
                                                       Never fulfil
                                                      A tyrant's will,
                                                   Nor willingly live a slave.

The addressee is almost enwrapped within this secular hymn, it is not one of praise or lamentation but of defiance. It was published just two weeks after the release of Jones from prison. We see alternating tercets rhymed aab between the speaker and The Chorus. The speaker had created an alternative ascension narrative with a revolutionary and proletarian goddess breaking free from the prison. The refrains from The Chorus are questionings and when they are given the new commandment:

> *Never fulfil*
> *A tyrant's will,*
> *Nor willingly live a slave.*

Rather than the Christian 'to love your enemies' they sing in unison a sextet abbabb of solidarity. This is an example of what Margret A. Loose called 'The Chartist Imaginary' which she defined as being: 'The political and the literary, for Chartism, were inexorable.'[81]

The failure of Chartism is correctly, in my view, diagnosed by O'Brien as a failure of a vacillating leadership.[82] A failure of

---

81   Loose, Margret A, *The Chartist Imaginary (Ohio, Ohio State University, 2014), p.3*

82   *O'Brien, (1995 pp.71-74).*

revolution in England, at that time claimed Marx, would make any revolution 'in Europe a storm in a teacup.'[83]However, O'Brien's position is contested by one of the leading scholars of Chartism, John Saville in his *1848 The British State and the Chartist movement*[84]. In particular the schema for the failure of 1848 to transmute into a revolutionary situation is contested. O'Brien does not cast aspersions on Feargus O'Connor's character or bravery. He made an error, as did others in the leadership. However, if the 'the Charter and something more' had succeeded. That would have been, by my analysis, a circumstance which would have provided the material base for the triumph of a British proletarian poetics and a massive boost to the international worker's movement. Saville argued two clear lines in his explanation for this catastrophe. To understand Chartism in 1848 we should:

'locate British domestic politics within the triangle of revolutionary Paris, insurgent Ireland, a revitalized Chartist movement in London and the industrial North.'[85]

I do not think many Marxists would disagree with him there. However, he continues that once the tide had ebbed in France and Ireland the Chartists were lost. No, that is to see it camera obscura for as Marx had argued above, England was the key to a successful continental revolution because of its higher development of Capital. Saville' second error is on the nature of revolution. While correctly criticising those theoreticians, who saw the demise of the worker's movement as one of being granted gradual concessions by the bourgeoisie.[86] He comprehends the coercive strength of the state apparatus as the concrete reason

83   Marx, Karl 'On Poland' *Marx/Engels Collected Works Vol. 6, p.389.*

84   *Savile, John 1848 The British State and the Chartist movement (Cambridge, Cambridge University Press 1990). p.1*

85   *Saville (1990) p.1*

86   *Barrington, Moore. Jr. Social Origins of Dictatorship and Democracy (Boston, Beacon Press, 1996) p.39.*

for the lack of a revolution. This meshes conveniently with his membership of the Communist Party of Great Britain who were advocating the parliamentary road to socialism in Britain at the time he was writing. Paradoxically there can be little doubt that in London in 1848 the ruling class thought revolution was in the air. The Duke of Wellington was called from retirement to lead the troops, 100,000 special constables were recruited from the ranks of the petty-bourgeoisie and the Royal Family were transferred to the Isle of Wight.

However, the masses did not simply retreat to their hovels and cottages afterwards. As Heaney, wrote in 1850:

> *In the past those Chartists who espoused socialist programmes had been denounced as" utopian" and "dangerous". But time has brought them to two alternatives: a retreat from the Charter into 'bourgeois idealism' or the bordering of the agitation to include socialist aims*[87]

An essential aspect of my argument is that 'labour' when not estranged from itself is the creative and collective expression of humanity and when given propitious circumstances i.e. communism it will develop into myriad forms with infinite possibilities thus, we can see the magnitude of the defeat of Chartism for labouring-class literature. I agree with Leon Trotsky that in the higher stages of communism:

> *The average human type will rise to the heights of an Aristotle, a Goethe, or a Marx. And above this ridge new peaks will rise.* [88]

So, I suggest, that when the masses are in a heightened state of class consciousness.

87   Schoen, A.R *The Chartist Challenge* (London, Heinemann, 1958) p 197 .

88   Trotsky, Leon, *Literature and Revolution* (London, Redwords, 1991), p. 284.

When the proletariat is a 'class-for-itself' (Marx) and aware of itself as the 'subject' of history then their potential for creativity is increased. We saw this during Chartism with poetry and will observe it in the early years after the Russian October 1917 revolution. I shall examine some of the ideas around this aesthetic in the conclusion. Thus, I have shown how the genres employed by the labouring classes are, in the last instance, moulded by the level of class struggle.

Finally, a poem by Gerald Massey.

THE MEN OF "FORTY-EIGHT."

They rose in Freedom's rare sunrise,
 Like giants roused from wine!
And in their hearts, and in their eyes,
 The God leapt up divine!
Their souls flashed out like naked swords,
 Unsheathed for fiery fate; —
Strength went like battle with their words,
 The men of Forty-eight.
   Hurrah!
For the men of Forty-eight.
 Dark days have fall'n! yet in the strife,
They bate no more sublime, —
 And bravely works the fiery life, —
Their hearts' pulse thro' the time.
 As grass is greenest trodden down,
So suffering makes men great;
 And this dark tide shall grandly crown
The men of forty-eight.
   Hurrah!
For the men of Forty-eight.
 Some, in a bloody burial sleep,

Like Greeks, to glory gone!
  Swift in their steps, avengers leap
With their proof armour on!
  And hearts beat high with dauntless trust,
We'll triumph soon or late,
  Though they be mouldering in the dust,
— Brave men of Forty-eight.
                    Hurrah!
For the men of Forty-eight!...
[...}
  Ye'll find them all elate, —
And true as ever Spartan band!
  The Men of Forty-eight.
                    Hurrah!
For the Men of Forty-eight.[89]

Two things about Massey's poem strike the reader. Firstly, its verbose language to describe the zenith of working-class struggle in Britain, there is a dissonance between subject and form. And secondly, his convolution of secular and sacred registers. In Massey's case unlike Jones, this does represent a genuine confusion for as (Randle 1999, p.190) illustrates he vacillated between militant labouring class poetry to be an apologist for British Imperialism. I argue that this was because having no systematic method he just reacted to events. Perhaps here we have the kernel of why the Bolsheviks created a situation where a revolution and therefore the material base for a proletarian poetics existed. Because Lenin affirmed 'without revolutionary theory, there can be no revolutionary practice.' The British working class by its very nature would have had 'combined and uneven consciousness.' This required not a loose network of newspapers publishing poetry. But a vanguard party with a full spectrum of publications both literary and political necessary if

---

89   *Massey, Gerald The Poetical Works Complete in One Volume. (Boston, Ticknor and Fields, 1857) p.103-104*

the Gramscian 'war of manoeuvre' was to be won which is the prerequisite for the victory of the social revolution. The latter being the requirement of a proletarian poetic.

CONCLUSION.

V.I. Lenin focused on the problems of the writer under capitalism. He suggested:

> *One cannot live in society and be free from society. The freedom of the bourgeois writer, artist or actress is simply masked (or hypocritically masked) dependence on the money-bag, on corruption...* [90]

Thus, as I suggested one must argue it is a consequence that for working-class writers, like the Chartists, to be free there must be a qualitatively different society.

> *The history of Chartist literature is not only a struggle for new subject matter but also a most complex search for a new literary method.*[91]

Therefore, I reiterate that a prerequisite for a proletarian poetic is the gaining of State power by the masses. Only then do the societal conditions exist to facilitate what Boris Arvatov called *Life-Building*. In this context Lenin continued his musing on the problems of literature:

> *(Ours) will be a free literature because of the idea of socialism and sympathy with the working people* [92].

The aesthetics of William Morris could be understood as an attempt to remove the division of labour between the artist or indeed poet, and manual labour. An attempt to reintroduce some of the lessons he had learnt from John Ruskin but from the standpoint of Socialism and is understood as an advance. It is of

---

90   *Lenin, V.I Collected Works Volume 10, Moscow, Progress Publishers, 1965, p. 68*

91   *Kovalev Y.V Victorian Studies Vol. 2, No. 2 (December 1958) p.126.*

92   *Lenin (1965), p.10,*

significance to note that Trotsky thought the conditions were not ripe for Boris Arvatov concept of *shiznestraitalstsn* (Life-building) which was the total decommodification and thus de-fetishization of the process of art and poetry which would take place in the 'means of production'. Art would become no different from any other form of labour. Boris Arvatov (2017 [1926], p.15) argued:

Art and life – how should these apparently heterogeneous phenomena be connected to each other? The question is a stumbling block in front of bourgeois science and bourgeois practice, unsolved and unsolvable in the conditions of capitalist society.

Hence this school competed with many others who were debating art and literature in the early days of the revolution and called themselves Productionists. With the ambitions of eradicating the artificial division of mental/physical labour. Or as Alexander Bogdanov *Proletarian* Poetry claimed, 'Is not the poet, the organizer of his class.' https://www.marxists.org/archive/bogdanov/1923/proletarianpoetry.htm . Bogdanov coined the term 'proletarian monism'. This is essential to understanding proletarian literature and art. Bogdanov thought 'collective labour' and the consciousness produced by it was the foundation for a proletarian poetics. He argued (1923 ibid) that it: 'embraced every aspect of a human and embracing all elements of experience'. Thus, it counterposed 'bourgeois dualism' where there is not this unity but division. He argued elsewhere:

To organize the forces in his social world, his struggle...the proletarian needs a new class art. The spirit of this art is the collectivisation of labour; it assimilates and reflects the world from the viewpoint of its feelings... its creative will...[93]

---

93   *Bogdanov, Alexander The Proletariat and Art Bowlt [Ed] Russian Art of the Avant-Garde (London, Thames & Hudson 2017) pp 176*

As I mentioned Lenin was arguing against this as early as 1920 as did Trotsky in *Literature and Revolution*, 1924. More generally it was cogently argued by both Lenin and Trotsky that because the class-conscious Russian proletariat had been decimated in three years of Civil War. Sixteen armies from Imperial powers fought on the side of the counter-revolutionaries. Although the revolution had been saved, but as Lenin argued in 1922 at a huge cost which was 'a worker's state without a working class.' This created the conditions which prefigured the Stalinist Gulags and Show Trials. Ultimately including the eradication of the Central Committee who had ordered the October 1917 insurrection, except for Stalin, by 1940. Arvatov was on the far-Left of the aesthetics Renaissance, which briefly flowered in the U.S.S.R. with *Prolecult*. Their ideas, in my view, were largely correct, but the objective conditions ultimately did not allow their implementation. Where does this leave the proletarian poetic aesthetic, Marxism? I agree with the poet Vladimir Mayakovsky, who worked for the revolutionary Left Front for the Arts. It must endeavour:

> *[to] re-examine the ideology and practices of so-called leftist art, and to abandon individualism to increase art's value for developing communism.*"[94]

My findings are therefore that, firstly there is a dialectical relationship between social class and poetry. Although this is complexified by the 'relatively autonomous' nature of the base to the superstructure. An example of this would be Raymond Williams' important contribution 'Base and Superstructure.'[95] We understand that they have a dialectical relation, interacting upon each other. I have shown a dialogue between Romanticism and early Chartist poetry noting the work of Janowitz (1998) and

---

94   *https://monoskop.org/LEF*

95   *Williams, Raymond. Base and Superstructure in Marxist Cultural Theory" New Left Review, no.82, 1973, p. 3.*

Sanders (2009). Also, I noted a change of genre and a change in the percentage of the numbers of Chartist and non- Chartist poets submitting work after the defeat of the 1842 General Strike. This led to the backward looking O'Connoirite Land Scheme. Chartism and its poetics were revived in 1848 giving a glimpse of what a proletarian aesthetic could resemble. The only occasion that there existed a material base for a labouring class poetics, I suggested, was the brief period following the October 1917 revolution until the counter-revolutionary and doctrinaire imposition of Socialist Realism upon the international workers' movement at the World Writers Congress in 1934. Once Stalin had proclaimed writers should be 'the engineers of the human soul.'[96] The phrase occurred in conversation between Stalin and Maxim Gorky on October 26th, 1932. Mayakovsky would commit suicide rather than become a mouthpiece for Stalin and his new ruling class.

I would suggest that an area of potential research would be a comparison of the writings of political prisoners during the Chartist period and those of Irish prisoners held as a result of 'The Troubles' 1969-1998. The primary sources for both exist. An analysis by genre, class composition and the relationship to the dominant poetics of each epoch may bear some interesting fruit when juxtaposed. One could imagine Ernest Jones and Bobby Sands as possible writers of both poetry and prose for comparison and analysis.[97] Or equally the prison poems of Victor Serge in the Stalinist gulag in 1933 come to mind as a possible alternative.[98] As well as his significant prose-fiction and other writings all available to the scholar. Although with Serge the question of translation would need to be answered. Also, of interest would be researching the largely neglected area of working-class women poets in the 19th century. I note the recent research of Florence

---

96   *Stalin, Collected Works, vol.13 (Moscow, 1953) p.410.*

97   *Sands, Bobby Writings from Prison (Cork, Mercier Press, 1988).*

98   *Serge, Victor Resistance (San Francisco, City Lights Books, 1989).*

Boos.[99] The movement of the oppressed in Britain has yet to gain the heights of the Paris Commune 1871, which Janowitz (1998) references, or that brief flowering in Russia 1917- 34 with its experiments in poetry and art. So finally, my analysis had considered two types of poetic. The Romantic which, although it employs the language of 'the ordinary people' is profoundly individualistic and the proletarian which is anti-individualistic but not against the individual. It is a multivoiced collectivity. I did find an echo of Romanticism in proletarian verse; indeed, it was the dominant cord until the defeat of the 1842 General Strike in Britain. Again, hope arose renewed with the victory of the October revolution in Russia and a blooming of all the arts until it's defeats at the hands of the Stalinist bureaucracy. I argue that the future of aesthetics resides in the tradition and spirit of Chartism and the October Revolution. Therefore, the future of humanity lies in the agency of the proletariat.

---

99   *Boos, Florence [ed] Working-Class Women Poets In Victorian Britain (Plymouth, Boordview Press, 2008).*

BIBLIOGRAPHY.

Primary Sources.

Arnold, Mathew *Literature and Dogma preface.*

https://hdl.handle.net/2027/uiug.30112073726298

Byron, Lord *The Major Works* (Oxford, Oxford University Press, 2008).

Cooper, Thomas *The Life of Thomas Cooper Written by Himself* (London, Hodder & Stoughton, 1873).

Cooper, Thomas *The Poetical Works of Thomas Cooper* (London, Hodder & Stoughton, 1877).

Cooper, Thomas *The Northern Star* (1841).

Engels, Friedrich *Dialectics of Nature* (Moscow, Progress Publishers, 1976).

Engels, Friedrich *Socialism: Utopian or Scientific* (London, Bookmarks, 1993).

Feuerbach, Ludwig *The Essence of Christianity*, George Eliot (Translator) (New York

Dover Philosophical Classics, 2008).

Frost, Thomas *Forty Years' Recollections: Literary and Political* (London: S. Low, Marston, Searle, and Rivington, 1880).

Gammage, R.C. *History of the chartist movement* (London, Merlin Press, (1976 [1894]).

Jones, Ernest *The Battle-Day and Other Poems* (London, Routledge & Co, 1855).

Jones, Ernest *The Labourer*,1846.

Jones, Ernest The Labourer vol 1, 1847.

Jones, Ernest (1847b) 'Literary Review', *The Labourer, vol* 2, 1847.

Harney, G. Julian The Red Republican & the Friend of the People. London: Merlin Press [etc.], https://catalog.hathitrust.org/Record/012289057

Keats, John, *The Complete Poems* (London, Penguin Classics, 1973).

London Corresponding Society, Nov 19th, 1794 (1795).

Karl, Marx & Frederick, Engels, *Collected Works, 50 vols, vol 3 published or in preparation* (London, 1975-n/a).

Marx, Karl & Engels, Frederick *Collected Works in 50 vols*, vol 4 (New York, International Publishers, 2004).

Marx, Karl *Early Writings* (London, Pelican Marx Library,1977).

Marx, Karl & Engels Frederick *Literature and Art: Selections from Their Writings* (New York, International Publishers, 1947).

Marx, Karl & Frederick Engels *On Britain* (Moscow, Foreign Languages Publishing House, 1953).

Marx, Karl. & Frederick Engels *On Literature and Art* (Moscow, Progress Publishers, 1976).

Marx and Engels *On the Trade Unions* (New York, International Publishers, 1987).

Marx, Karl. & Frederick Engels *Selected Correspondence, 1846-1895 Marxist Library, 29,* (New York, International Publishers 1942).

Marx, Karl. & Frederick Engels *Selected Correspondence* (Moscow, Progress Publishers, 1965).

Reminiscences of Marx and Engels (Moscow, Foreign Languages Publishing House, 1963).

Karl, Marx & Frederick Engels *The German Ideology* (London, Lawrence & Wishart, 1982). https://www.marxists.org/archive/marx/works/1852/18th-brumaire/ch01.htm

The Marx-Engels Correspondence, *The Personal Letters, 1844-1877.* (London, Weidenfeld and Nicolson, 1981).

Massey, Gerald *The Poetical Works in One Volume,* (Boston, Ticknor & Fields M CCC LVII).

Mill, John Stuart. "Thoughts on Poetry and Its Varieties." *(The Crayon,* vol. 7, no. 4, 1860).

Morris, William *Useful Work v, Useless Toil* (London, Penguin Books, Great Ideas, 2008).

Rousseau, Jean-Jacques. *On the Social Contract* (New York, Dover Thrift Editions, 2016).

Ruskin, John *Selected Writings* (Oxford, Oxford University Press, 2009).

Shelley, Percy Bysshe, *The Major Works* (Oxford, Oxford University Press, 2003).

Tennyson, Alfred, *The Major Works* (Oxford, Oxford University Press, 2009).

The Chartist Circular, By permission of the British Library Board.

The Northern Star and the Leeds General Advertiser British Library Newspapers & Periodicals:

http://find.galegroup.com.libezproxy.open.ac.uk/bncn/start.
do?prodId=BNCN&userGroupName=tou&finalAuth=true

Wordsworth, William *Letters of William Wordsworth: a
new selection* [Ed] Alan G. Hill. (Oxford, Oxford University
Press, 1984).

Wordsworth, William. *The letters of William and Dorothy
Wordsworth: The later Years, 1821-1853* (2nd Ed.) (Vols. 1-4).
(Oxford, Oxford University Press, 1978-1988).

Wordsworth, William. *Wordsworth's Political Writings (Kindle
Edition).*

Wordsworth, William *The Major Works* (Oxford, Oxford
University Press, 2000).

SECONDARY SOURCES.

Althusser, Louis *Lenin and Philosophy and other essays* (India, Akkar Books, 2006).

Allen, Joan and Ashton. A. Owen [ed] *Papers for The People A Study of the Chartist Press* (London, The Merlin Press, 2005).

Arvon, Henri *Marxist Esthetics* (London, Cornell Press, 1973).

Arvatov, Boris *Art & Production* (London, Pluto Press, 2017[1926]).

Barrington, Moore. Jr. *Social Origins of Dictatorship and Democracy* (Boston, Beacon Press, 1996).

Black, David *Helen Macfarlane* (New York, Lexington Books, 2004).

Blair, K & Mina, G [ed] *Class and Canon, Labouring-Class Poetry and Politics 1750- 1900* (London, Palgrave Macmillan, 2013).

Benjamin, Walter *The Work of Art in the Age of Mechanical Reproduction* (London, Penguin Great Ideas, 2008 [1936]).

Bogdanov, Alexandr www.marxists.org/archive/bogdanov/1923/proletarianpoetry.htm

Bogdanov, Alexandr The Proletariat and Art *in* Bowlt [ed*] Russian Art of the Avant- Garde* (London, Thames & Hudson 2017).

Boos, Florence [ed] *Working-Class Women Poets In Victorian Britain* (Plymouth, Boordview Press, 2008).

Bowlt, John E [ed]. *Russia Art of the Avant-Garde* (London, Thames & Hudson, 2017). Brecht, Bertolt, in *Paulo Freire: A*

Critical Encounter (1993) by Peter McLaren and Peter Leonard (London, Routledge, 1992).

Briggs, Asa *Chartism* (Stroud, Sutton Publishing,1998).

Caudwell, Christopher, *Illusion and Reality* (Lawrence & Wishart, 1973 [1937).

Caudwell, Christopher *Culture as Politics* (Pluto Press, London, 2018).

Chandler, James K *Wordsworth's Second Nature: A Study in the Poetry and Politics* (Chicago, University of Chicago Press, 1984).

Chase, Malcolm *Chartism A New History* (Manchester, Manchester University Press, 2007).

Charlton, John *The Chartists: The First National Workers' Movement* (London: Pluto Press, 1997).

Cunningham, Valentine *Victorian Poets: A Critical Reader* (Oxford, Wiley Blackwell, 2014).

Eagleton, Terry *Literary Theory: An Introduction* (Oxford, Blackwell, 1996).

Eagleton, Terry *Marxism and Literary Criticism* (London, Routledge Classics 2008),

Epstein, James *The Lion of Freedom* (London, Breviary Stuff Publications, 2015).

Foot, Paul, *The Vote* (London, Bookmarks, 2012).

Goodridge, John: https://lcpoets.wordpress.com/introtobibliography/

Goodway, David *London Chartism 1838-1848* (Cambridge, Cambridge University Press, 1982).

Goodway, David *George Julian Harney: The Chartists were Right.* (London, Merlin Press, 2015).

Gramsci, Antonio 'The Formation of Intellectuals' in *The Modern Prince and Other Writings (New York, International Publishers, 1978).*

Gramsci, Antonio *Selections from the Prison Notebooks.* (London, Lawrence and Wishart, 1982).

Groves, Reg *But we shall rise again: A narrative history of Chartism* (London, Secker and Warburg, 1938).

Karlin Daniel. [Ed] *The Penguin Book of Victorian Verse* (Penguin Classics), Penguin Books Ltd. Kindle Edition.

Kovalev, Y. *An anthology of Chartist Literature* (Moscow, Foreign Languages Publishing House,1956).

Kovalev, Y. *Victorian Studies Vol. 2*, No. 2 (December 1958).

Krantz, Mark *The 1842 General Strike* (London, Bookmarks, 2014).

Krishnamurthy, Arura *The Working-Class Intellectual in Eighteenth-and Nineteenth- Century Britain* (London, Taylor & Francis, 2009).

Hall, Robert, G *Voices of the People,* (Wales, Merlin Press, 2007).

Hartmann, Geoffrey *Wordsworth Poetry 1787-1814* (London, Yale University Press, 1974).

Haywood, Ian [ed] *The Literature of Struggle: An Anthology of Chartist Fiction* (London, Routledge, 1995).

Hemingway, Andrew *Marxism and the History of Art* (London, Pluto Press, 2006).

Janowitz, Anne *Lyric and Labour in the Romantic tradition*, (Cambridge, Cambridge University Press, 1998).

Jenkins, Mike *The General Strike of 1842* (London, Lawrence & Wishart, 1980).

Johnson, Pauline *Marxist Aesthetics*, (London, Routledge Revivals, 1984).

Lenin, V.I *Collected Works Vol 10*, (Moscow, Progress Publishers, 1965).

Lenin, V.I. *Collected Works Vol 30* (Moscow, Progress Publishers, 1965).

Loose, Margaret. A *The Chartist Imaginary: Literary Form in Working-Class Political Theory and Practice.* (Ohio, Ohio State University Press, 2016).

Lukács György *History & Class Consciousness: Studies in Marxist Dialectics,* (Pontypool, The Merlin Press, 2010).

Mahamdallie, Hassan '*Crossing the river of fire: the socialism of William Morris* (London, Redwords, 2008).

Murphy. Paul, Thomas, *Towards a Working-Class Canon*, (Ohio, Ohio State University Press, 1994).

O'Brien, Mark '*Perish the Privileged Orders', A Socialist History of The Chartist Movement,* (London, Redwords, 1995).

O'Gorman, Francis, *Victorian Poetry: The Annotated Edition* (Oxford, Blackwell, 2017)

Sanders, Mike *The Poetry of Chartism: Aesthetics, Politics, History* (Cambridge, Cambridge University Press, 2009).

Sands, Bobby *Writings from Prison* (Cork, Mercier Press, 1988).

Saville, John 1848 *The British State and the Chartist movement* (Cambridge, Cambridge University Press, 1990).

Saville, John *Ernest Jones Chartist* (London, Lawrence & Wishart, 1952).

Scheckner, Peter *An Anthology of Chartist Poetry 1830s-1850s* (London, Associated University Press, 1989).

Schoen, A.R *The Chartist Challenge* (London, Heinemann, 1958).

Schwab, Ulrich *The poetry of the Chartist Movement: A Literary and Historical Study* (Dordrecht, Kluwer Academic Publishers, 1987).

Serge, Victor *Resistance* (San Francisco, City Lights Books, 1989).

Stalin, *Collected Works*, vol.13 (Moscow, 1953).

Stedman-Jones, Gareth *Languages of Class: Studies in English Working-Class History 1832-1982* (Cambridge, Cambridge University Press, 2008).

Rose, Johnathan, *The Intellectual Life of the Working Class* (London, Yale University Press, 2001).

Randle, Tim Chartist Poetry and Song in *The Chartist Legacy* (United Kingdom, Merlin Press, 1999).

Rennie, Simon *The Poetry of Ernest Jones: Myth, Song and the 'Mighty Mind'* (London, Routledge, 2016).

Royle, Edward, *Chartism* (London, Longman, 1996).

Royle, Edward, *Revolutionary Britannia?* (Manchester, Manchester University Press, 2000).

Taylor, Miles *Ernest* Jones, *Chartism and the Romance of Politics 1819-1869* (Oxford, Oxford University Press, 2003).

Trotsky, Leon, *Literature and Revolution* (London, Redwords, 1991).

Trotsky, Leon, *Leon Trotsky On Britain* (New York, Pathfinder, 2012).

Thompson, Dorothy, *The Chartists* (London, Breviary Stuff Publishers, 2013).

Thompson, Dorothy, *The Dignity of Chartism* (London, Verso, 2015).

Thompson, E.P, *The Making of the English Working Classes* (Harmondsworth, Penguin, 1965).

Vicinus, Martha, *The Industrial Muse: A Study of Nineteenth Century Working-Class Literature* (London, Croom Helm, 1974).

Williams, John *Wordsworth: romantic poetry and revolution* (Manchester, Manchester University Press, 1989).

Williams, Raymond. *Base and Superstructure in Marxist Cultural Theory* New Left Review, no. 82, 1973.

Williams, Raymond, *Culture and Society 1780-1950* (London)